Art created by Desaree Jones

Journal created by:
Ranada Dalton
MHC, LPC, MAMFT, Certified Sexologist, Certified Inclusive Sex Coach

www.empoweredlivinginc.net
www.beautifullyhuman.net

Date_____

Dear Me,

_____
_____
_____
_____
_____
_____
_____
_____
_____
_____
_____
_____

d a picture of yourself

_____
_____
_____
_____
_____

Sincerely,

Body check in

DATE _____

HOW DOES YOUR BODY FEEL
PHYSICALLY, EMOTIONALLY, &
MENTALLY?
_____

THINGS I LIKE ABOUT IT
- _____
- _____
- _____
- _____

WHAT CAN I DO TO BE A GOOD
STEWARD TO MY BODY?
_____

WHAT DO I FIND SEXY ABOUT ME
_____

I'M GRATEFUL MY BODY...

HOW DOES MY BODY MAKE ME
FEEL (ONE WORD)?
_____

I'm feeling inspired to

Body check in

DATE

HOW DOES YOUR BODY FEEL PHYSICALLY, EMOTIONALLY, & MENTALLY?

THINGS I LIKE ABOUT IT
-
-
-
-

WHAT CAN I DO TO BE A GOOD STEWARD TO MY BODY?

WHAT DO I FIND SEXY ABOUT ME

I'M GRATEFUL MY BODY...

HOW DOES MY BODY MAKE ME FEEL (ONE WORD)?

Body check in

DATE
_____

HOW DOES YOUR BODY FEEL PHYSICALLY, EMOTIONALLY, & MENTALLY?
_____

THINGS I LIKE ABOUT IT
- _____
- _____
- _____
- _____

WHAT CAN I DO TO BE A GOOD STEWARD TO MY BODY?
_____

WHAT DO I FIND SEXY ABOUT ME
_____

I'M GRATEFUL MY BODY...
_____

HOW DOES MY BODY MAKE ME FEEL (ONE WORD)?
_____

Body check in

DATE

HOW DOES YOUR BODY FEEL PHYSICALLY, EMOTIONALLY, & MENTALLY?

THINGS I LIKE ABOUT IT
-
-
-
-

WHAT CAN I DO TO BE A GOOD STEWARD TO MY BODY?

WHAT DO I FIND SEXY ABOUT ME

I'M GRATEFUL MY BODY...

HOW DOES MY BODY MAKE ME FEEL (ONE WORD)?

Body check in

DATE

HOW DOES YOUR BODY FEEL PHYSICALLY, EMOTIONALLY, & MENTALLY?

THINGS I LIKE ABOUT IT
-
-
-
-

WHAT CAN I DO TO BE A GOOD STEWARD TO MY BODY?

WHAT DO I FIND SEXY ABOUT ME

I'M GRATEFUL MY BODY…

HOW DOES MY BODY MAKE ME FEEL (ONE WORD)?

Body check in

DATE

HOW DOES YOUR BODY FEEL PHYSICALLY, EMOTIONALLY, & MENTALLY?

THINGS I LIKE ABOUT IT
-
-
-
-

WHAT CAN I DO TO BE A GOOD STEWARD TO MY BODY?

WHAT DO I FIND SEXY ABOUT ME

I'M GRATEFUL MY BODY...

HOW DOES MY BODY MAKE ME FEEL (ONE WORD)?

Body check in

DATE

HOW DOES YOUR BODY FEEL PHYSICALLY, EMOTIONALLY, & MENTALLY?

THINGS I LIKE ABOUT IT
-
-
-
-

WHAT CAN I DO TO BE A GOOD STEWARD TO MY BODY?

WHAT DO I FIND SEXY ABOUT ME

I'M GRATEFUL MY BODY...

HOW DOES MY BODY MAKE ME FEEL (ONE WORD)?

Body check in

DATE

HOW DOES YOUR BODY FEEL PHYSICALLY, EMOTIONALLY, & MENTALLY?

THINGS I LIKE ABOUT IT
-
-
-
-

WHAT CAN I DO TO BE A GOOD STEWARD TO MY BODY?

WHAT DO I FIND SEXY ABOUT ME

I'M GRATEFUL MY BODY...

HOW DOES MY BODY MAKE ME FEEL (ONE WORD)?

Body check in

DATE

HOW DOES YOUR BODY FEEL PHYSICALLY, EMOTIONALLY, & MENTALLY?

THINGS I LIKE ABOUT IT
-
-
-
-

WHAT CAN I DO TO BE A GOOD STEWARD TO MY BODY?

WHAT DO I FIND SEXY ABOUT ME

I'M GRATEFUL MY BODY...

HOW DOES MY BODY MAKE ME FEEL (ONE WORD)?

Body check in

DATE

HOW DOES YOUR BODY FEEL PHYSICALLY, EMOTIONALLY, & MENTALLY?

THINGS I LIKE ABOUT IT
-
-
-
-

WHAT CAN I DO TO BE A GOOD STEWARD TO MY BODY?

WHAT DO I FIND SEXY ABOUT ME

I'M GRATEFUL MY BODY...

HOW DOES MY BODY MAKE ME FEEL (ONE WORD)?

Body check in

DATE

HOW DOES YOUR BODY FEEL PHYSICALLY, EMOTIONALLY, & MENTALLY?

THINGS I LIKE ABOUT IT
-
-
-
-

WHAT CAN I DO TO BE A GOOD STEWARD TO MY BODY?

WHAT DO I FIND SEXY ABOUT ME

I'M GRATEFUL MY BODY...

HOW DOES MY BODY MAKE ME FEEL (ONE WORD)?

Body check in

DATE

HOW DOES YOUR BODY FEEL PHYSICALLY, EMOTIONALLY, & MENTALLY?

THINGS I LIKE ABOUT IT
-
-
-
-

WHAT CAN I DO TO BE A GOOD STEWARD TO MY BODY?

WHAT DO I FIND SEXY ABOUT ME

I'M GRATEFUL MY BODY...

HOW DOES MY BODY MAKE ME FEEL (ONE WORD)?

Body check in

DATE

HOW DOES YOUR BODY FEEL PHYSICALLY, EMOTIONALLY, & MENTALLY?

THINGS I LIKE ABOUT IT
- _____
- _____
- _____
- _____

WHAT CAN I DO TO BE A GOOD STEWARD TO MY BODY?

WHAT DO I FIND SEXY ABOUT ME

I'M GRATEFUL MY BODY...

HOW DOES MY BODY MAKE ME FEEL (ONE WORD)?

Body check in

DATE

HOW DOES YOUR BODY FEEL PHYSICALLY, EMOTIONALLY, & MENTALLY?

THINGS I LIKE ABOUT IT
-
-
-
-

WHAT CAN I DO TO BE A GOOD STEWARD TO MY BODY?

WHAT DO I FIND SEXY ABOUT ME

I'M GRATEFUL MY BODY...

HOW DOES MY BODY MAKE ME FEEL (ONE WORD)?

Body check in

DATE

HOW DOES YOUR BODY FEEL
PHYSICALLY, EMOTIONALLY, &
MENTALLY?

THINGS I LIKE ABOUT IT
-
-
-
-

WHAT CAN I DO TO BE A GOOD
STEWARD TO MY BODY?

WHAT DO I FIND SEXY ABOUT ME

I'M GRATEFUL MY BODY...

HOW DOES MY BODY MAKE ME
FEEL (ONE WORD)?

Body check in

DATE

HOW DOES YOUR BODY FEEL PHYSICALLY, EMOTIONALLY, & MENTALLY?

THINGS I LIKE ABOUT IT
-
-
-
-

WHAT CAN I DO TO BE A GOOD STEWARD TO MY BODY?

WHAT DO I FIND SEXY ABOUT ME

I'M GRATEFUL MY BODY...

HOW DOES MY BODY MAKE ME FEEL (ONE WORD)?

Body check in

DATE

HOW DOES YOUR BODY FEEL PHYSICALLY, EMOTIONALLY, & MENTALLY?

THINGS I LIKE ABOUT IT
-
-
-
-

WHAT CAN I DO TO BE A GOOD STEWARD TO MY BODY?

WHAT DO I FIND SEXY ABOUT ME

I'M GRATEFUL MY BODY...

HOW DOES MY BODY MAKE ME FEEL (ONE WORD)?

Body check in

DATE

HOW DOES YOUR BODY FEEL PHYSICALLY, EMOTIONALLY, & MENTALLY?

THINGS I LIKE ABOUT IT
-
-
-
-

WHAT CAN I DO TO BE A GOOD STEWARD TO MY BODY?

WHAT DO I FIND SEXY ABOUT ME

I'M GRATEFUL MY BODY...

HOW DOES MY BODY MAKE ME FEEL (ONE WORD)?

Body check in

DATE
_____

HOW DOES YOUR BODY FEEL PHYSICALLY, EMOTIONALLY, & MENTALLY?
_____

THINGS I LIKE ABOUT IT
- _____
- _____
- _____
- _____

WHAT CAN I DO TO BE A GOOD STEWARD TO MY BODY?
_____

WHAT DO I FIND SEXY ABOUT ME
_____

I'M GRATEFUL MY BODY...
_____

HOW DOES MY BODY MAKE ME FEEL (ONE WORD)?
_____

Body check in

DATE

HOW DOES YOUR BODY FEEL PHYSICALLY, EMOTIONALLY, & MENTALLY?

THINGS I LIKE ABOUT IT
-
-
-
-

WHAT CAN I DO TO BE A GOOD STEWARD TO MY BODY?

WHAT DO I FIND SEXY ABOUT ME

I'M GRATEFUL MY BODY...

HOW DOES MY BODY MAKE ME FEEL (ONE WORD)?

Body check in

DATE
_____

HOW DOES YOUR BODY FEEL PHYSICALLY, EMOTIONALLY, & MENTALLY?
_____

THINGS I LIKE ABOUT IT
- _____
- _____
- _____
- _____

WHAT CAN I DO TO BE A GOOD STEWARD TO MY BODY?
_____

WHAT DO I FIND SEXY ABOUT ME
_____

I'M GRATEFUL MY BODY...
_____

HOW DOES MY BODY MAKE ME FEEL (ONE WORD)?
_____

Body check in

DATE

HOW DOES YOUR BODY FEEL PHYSICALLY, EMOTIONALLY, & MENTALLY?

THINGS I LIKE ABOUT IT
-
-
-
-

WHAT CAN I DO TO BE A GOOD STEWARD TO MY BODY?

WHAT DO I FIND SEXY ABOUT ME

I'M GRATEFUL MY BODY...

HOW DOES MY BODY MAKE ME FEEL (ONE WORD)?

Body check in

DATE

HOW DOES YOUR BODY FEEL PHYSICALLY, EMOTIONALLY, & MENTALLY?

THINGS I LIKE ABOUT IT
- _____
- _____
- _____
- _____

WHAT CAN I DO TO BE A GOOD STEWARD TO MY BODY?

WHAT DO I FIND SEXY ABOUT ME

I'M GRATEFUL MY BODY...

HOW DOES MY BODY MAKE ME FEEL (ONE WORD)?

Body check in

DATE

HOW DOES YOUR BODY FEEL PHYSICALLY, EMOTIONALLY, & MENTALLY?

THINGS I LIKE ABOUT IT
-
-
-
-

WHAT CAN I DO TO BE A GOOD STEWARD TO MY BODY?

WHAT DO I FIND SEXY ABOUT ME

I'M GRATEFUL MY BODY...

HOW DOES MY BODY MAKE ME FEEL (ONE WORD)?

I'm feeling inspired to

I'm feeling inspired to

I'm feeling inspired to

I'm feeling inspired to

I'm feeling inspired to

I'm feeling inspired to

I'm feeling inspired to

I'm feeling inspired to

I'm feeling inspired to

I'm feeling inspired to

I'm feeling inspired to

I'm feeling inspired to

I'm feeling inspired to

I'm feeling inspired to

I'm feeling inspired to

....
....
....
....
....
....
....
....
....
....
....
....
....
....
....
....
....
....

I'm feeling inspired to

I'm feeling inspired to

I'm feeling inspired to

I'm feeling inspired to

I'm feeling inspired to

I'm feeling inspired to

I'm feeling inspired to

I'm feeling inspired to